Love Roses & Thorns

Alicia Peat

BookLeaf
Publishing

India | USA | UK

Presentation by *BookLeaf Publishing*

Web: www.bookleafpub.com

E-mail: info@bookleafpub.com

ISBN: 9789363300309

First edition 2024

To my daughter may you love fully without fear
an love fully with strengthen

Flowers

She fell for the ones who gave her the flowers
Not aware of their thorns
She was adored
Who knew they leave her torn
Delicate as she held the flowers
They held her heart
One more precious then another
She fell for the ones who gave her the flowers
Not aware of thier thorns
A familiar love she now mourns
Elegant as she was as roses are
She will bloom again as flowers do

Selfless love

Selfless falling for love an all of loves
imperfections
Self reflections mirrors only show imperfections
Self love devotion to my commotion
Lost in this emotion
Reckless how I love you endless
Trying to mend this
Hopeful of love yet you leave me empty
Yet I have given plenty
Shall love you give shall be mines to keep
mend what you taken
I was mistaken that your love was mine
Love was only on borrowed time

Old love

Your like fresh air I'm dying to breath your
unaware that I'm here in the cracks of the
sidewalks near our coffee shop in the leaves that
dust of your shoulder I'm shadowing your
sunlight I'm the holes of your sweater left
hanging on a fence the crisp smoke of a
Marlboro the folded ticket to a bus pass no
longer used just red yarn lingering on your wrist
I'm here darling the skid marks on your shoes
crossing red lights your moon turning blue i
never left here still I haunt in the things that
remind me of a time a time I shared with you

Ache

Do You love the way I hurt
Do you lavish in my tears
 Did you kiss her to hurt me
Did you love her to kill me
If you knew what every touch of her would do to
me
Did you push into her to rip everything out of
me
Did you make her laugh to here me Cry was it
music to your ears
Did you dance with her
all for the love of me to die
 Do you love the way I hurt

Made by love

Love made me this way it gave me a black hole
for a heart to consume all of you into me
Love gave me mirrors for eyes I only see the
surface of your beauty I cannot see flaws Love
made me with hands strong to carry your
baggage
Love gave me arms to open wide as the ocean
and tides to pull u in
love handcrafted me for you so that our souls
would align and fingertips touch as our hands
correspond like a melody we dance to
Love gave me just enough of what u desire an
enough to inspire more
 Love made me for you and love gave me you

Abused

Love is abused
Kisses of black an blue
Bruised
Love is misused
Love is over used
Love is lies mistaken for truth
Love made me a fool
Heart over head
Love has fallen apart
All for the sake of you
Taken love for granted
Love can become damaged

Thorns

Things of beauty so delicate
Yet beware how she blooms
Her thorns her protection
For those who take with ill intention
A rose among daisies
Red rose lips speak with pure intent
She's weathered through storms
As petals will fall
Love her or love her not
She blooms
With every imperfection
Petals and thorns
She is perfection

Vines

There's vines keeping me tied
Your like leaves free falling
You spread your seed an I watched me become
less of you
I'm getting strangled
The vines choke
I am not woke
Tangled in lies
My lovers demise
I cannot bloom
You've neglected your rose
For a garden an hose
Theses vines have thorns
This love left me torn

Warning signs

You poured salt in my wounds yet convinced me
it was sugar
Oh how lips of honey get you stung by bees
Picking roses with thorns
I bleed
 Into your cup half full never enough
Liquor on your tongue
Never sober for telling truths
Nights in shades of black an blue
Can't recall the abuse
Clouds of your cigarette smoke
I choke
Hands on throat
Yet I spoke

The "I love you's" we forgot to say

Years left behind
A keepsake box of memories
Maybe we aged
Maybe we grew
Something familiar in you
some loves are ageless
As the distance ranges
If our memories get faded like photographs
If times of laughter leave us too fast
Forever a shared past
Regret less
relentless to ever end this
Dearest's truest
Friend
A long live love to the end
Although it never yield's to be said
I love you

The sins of you

I shall not envy whom you do not love
Your desires
Lustful inquiries
For it is love I ache
Your a void
Consumed with pleasures
You shall never know true treasures
Wounded as you are
My body cannot shield
You'll forever thirst
As she may be giving
She neither
will be fulfilling
I shall not envy your touch
Your lips
Your hands
Your …
Hips
What I long for
You cannot give
Love is gentle
Love is kind
Love is beautiful
Even when blind
Before two bodies become intertwined

Mothers love

Traps in these walls a place so familiar it feels
like home but cannot leave
These doors have locks
but no key
Why dose love come with pain
Why dose an umbilical cord feel like a chain
I try an fly like birds in their nest only to see my
wings have been clipped
Love is possessive sometimes the ones we love
become obsessive
Why dose parts of me feel like the parts of you
I don't want them too
Why do family trees grow roots
I wanna be like the leaves change and grow then
go
When a mothers heart no longer feels like home

Forevers

Forevers are promised
But not honest
If I shall be so modest to owe myself truths
I know your heart will fade
Feelings of love will age as our bodies do
Your lips will forget soft kisses
As sun comes to a haze in summer days our love
will change with seasons
May I still be the reason you stay forever
Even if forever can't be promised
To be honest
I know storms will rage on yet still I'll love you
In anger
In sadness
In the midst of my madness
If not forever
Then whenever

The affair

Her lips imprinted on your neck
Marks of a beast I shall slay
Her name spoken upon your lips give shivers to
my skin , bones and body
How shallow of a man to awaken love yet taunt
a women in mourning
She is not yours nor am I
He who belongs himself to everyone is for no
one
Yet I envy the nerve of her to love a borrowed
man
As I shall pity us the fool
Nor I or you hold a crown upon our heads
He's no king
He is of beast
No amount of women would make him be

As I am

I come in the shades of a garden
Red as roses bold an true
My lips soft spoke as I speak to you
I come in the shades of a garden
Dirt brown as my roots hold me to the ground
For my ancestors are proud
I come in the shades of a garden
I bloom in every season without reason
I've weathered storms made for my destruction
I am the flower
My seeds shall prosper
My offspring's will flourish in the love i endure
I am the flower I am the garden I am eve

Store flowers

I buy myself roses
The dandelion
An daisy's
I look at a familiar reflection
Her eyes reflecting mine
The beauty in her smile
Been awhile
Counting petals off of daisies
Do I love me
Do I love me not
Do I love me
Do I love me not
Oh how I must of forgot
As the petals fall from the last dying rose
I' again to must never forget to nurture the
beauty within
For I like the roses
The dandelions
An daisies
Will bloom

Thorns an kisses

Roses made for apologies
Your lips never mutter words of sorry
Your kisses silence me
Relentlessly my voice shouts in my mind
It is myself I have yet to find
Yet your hands seem to find my body trace scars
I do not remember
But they are known to you
The roses have grown an bloomed
Years have past I am fond of you
Is this déjà vu a familiar pain aches as I say
I love you
As you hand me the roses
Thorns and kisses

Baggage claim

For every love I've lost before you
I folded the memories in the back pocket of blue
jeans
Something old something new and something
blue
I packed away the past mistakes shoved into
luggage ripping at the seems
My carryon left of the things I've forgotten
along the journey my sanity an keys both left at
the door way
Yet you accompany me along a unknown
destination
You carry empty handed
Left with you baggage for my name to claim
Just enough room for you and for me
As I unpack my damaged
Stained of the scars from yesterday
Unwashed an clothed in my pain
Yet as you claim my heavy weight
Unload these traumas behind us now
Repack with the memories yet to come from a
new love we share now

Forgive love to be loved

As love once was my heart has changed
You've rearranged the words love
The meaning conflicted with pain
What once was pure your intent has changed
Love is not attention
Love is not affection nor attachment
Love is not superficial
The love you gave was only beneficial
I forgive you for that may be the only love
you've known
For i forgive myself for not finding the love
within
I forgive love for scars an broken hearts
I forgive love to give love
To be loved again

Love ,roses & thorns

Bittersweet as love may be
Bold in blooms of roses
Rose red like lips
Lips that speak of poetry
Oh how broken hearts speak so freely
Speak like art
Delicate as petals may fall
How the seasons change me oh how I weatherd
storms like roses in a garden
Dying
Yet I bloom in due time
Scars
As thorns draw more blood then one willing to
give
Oh how beautiful things tend to hurt when least
expected
Like love
Like roses & thorns

Him

To whom this may concern
Know your actions have left scars
Your words caused a war
Your lips kiss of posion
She to will have the same fate as I for all lies
lead to a demise
Know your heart is as broken as what you reap
onto the hearts you shattered
If hearts were glass your reflection is of
imperfection
Truly the enemy was your lack of self affection
My heart as it may be at a dismay
But yours will always betray you
Self sabotage a love for lust
Your true weakness a lack of trust
I hope you morn the death of us